Professionalism and Ethics

Professionalism and Ethics

A guide for dental care professionals

Fiona Stuart-Wilson

UMD Professional Ltd

QUAY
BOOKS

A division of MA Healthcare Ltd

Quay Books Division, MA Healthcare Ltd, St Jude's Church, Dulwich Road, London
SE24 0PB

British Library Cataloguing-in-Publication Data
A catalogue record is available for this book

© MA Healthcare Limited 2009

ISBN-10: 1 85642 381 6
ISBN-13: 978 1 85642 381 6

Printed by CLE, St Ives, Huntingdon, Cambridgeshire

Contents

Preface

This book has come about as a result of a series of articles written for *Dental Nursing* and I am indebted to the Editor of that journal, Andrea Porter, not just for commissioning the series in the first place, but in so doing for opening a door for me to explore the fascinating and perplexing subject of professionalism.

This book is not intended as a definitive text on professionalism, if such a thing could even exist. Professionalism and our society's view of it are evolving concepts, and they will continue to evolve over the coming years as our view of healthcare, and the role and rights of the patient, change. Rather, this volume is a personal reflection on the nature of professionalism and how it relates to the profession of dental nursing. In some ways professionalism is in the eye of the beholder, and to an extent I have enjoyed since the late 1980s a privileged grandstand view as the story of dental nursing as a profession has been played out. My observations are those of the interested lay person wishing to be informed rather than the immersed professional needing to know. The intention of this book therefore is to challenge thought and stimulate debate on what I believe is an essential subject for all dental nurses to embrace – what it means to be a professional.

Many people have assisted in the writing of this book in many different ways but the practical assistance offered by Mike Grace and Penny Parry in particular should not go without mention.

I must also acknowledge the unwitting input of the many hundreds of dental nurses I have met over the last two decades, who have provided me with many insights into the nature of their work and professional relationships, and from whom I have learned so much.

Professionalism is a constant choice, and there are challenges ahead in dental nurses being accepted as professionals and also in understanding and upholding the GDC's Standards. However, few I hope would argue that dental nursing is a responsible, skilled and worthwhile occupation and that it is important to develop and maintain public confidence. 2008 represented a major shift in the status and standing of the dental nurse, and developing professionalism is, I believe, something that all dental nurses owe not just to their profession but also to themselves.

Fiona Stuart-Wilson
July 2009

CHAPTER I

Introduction

The date 31 July 2008 marked a turning point in the working lives of current and future dental nurses all over the UK. From that date, all individuals wishing to work as a dental nurse must either be enrolled on a recognised training programme or registered with the General Dental Council (GDC). Although this is now common knowledge, what might be less evident is what registration really means and what responsibilities the dental nurse takes on with registration. The registered dental nurse becomes a dental care professional. But what does this mean? And what does professionalism actually mean?

This book explores the idea of professionalism and its practical implications for the dental nurse. Professionalism, as we shall see, is not a cut and dried idea or concept, with clear-cut answers to tricky questions. Professionalism and ethics are closely allied, and professionalism also involves, amongst other things, exercising judgement.

Perhaps a good place to start is to answer the question 'How did we get to this point?'.

The Dental Care Professional (DCP) registers actually opened on 31 July 2006, some 22 years after the BADN (or the Association of British Dental Surgery Assistants as it was then known) opened the Voluntary National Register (VNR) of dental nurses. That date saw the culmination of a protracted development and consultative process, involving different governments and an assortment of different organisations in dentistry, to reach agreement on the required legislation to allow registration.

Probably one of the most influential reports which helped to move registration forward was the Nuffield Report on the Education and Training of Personnel Auxiliary to Dentistry, published in 1993. At that time dental care professionals were termed auxiliaries; this report made recommendations to increase the range of the skills mix available to the dental team, with a dentist involving appropriately trained staff to increase efficiency and orientate services towards prevention. We have seen some of the effects of that report in the introduction of compulsory registration of dental nurses. Other factors which have had an impact on dental nurse registration could not perhaps have been foreseen; for example, the necessity of ensuring the safeguarding of patients highlighted in the various findings of the Shipman Inquiry is one such factor, but so too has been the further development of the dental nursing training curriculum.

The BADN published a response to the Nuffield Report in support of the Inquiry's proposal in 1994. Other dental organisations also published responses, but interestingly at that stage not all were in favour of dental nurse registration. The following year the GDC published its own consultation document, which heralded the beginning of the next stage.

1996 saw Dame Margaret Seward, then the President of the GDC, form the Dental Auxiliary Review Group (DARG), which brought together all interested organisations to discuss registration.

In 1998 DARG concluded that dental nurses should be registered with the GDC. The following year, the GDC made the formal decision in principle to register dental nurses and other Dental Care professional groups hitherto not registered, as part of a wider move to raise the standards of education and training of Dental Care Professionals (DCPs) through registration, but it was not until 2006 that the first dental nurse registered with the GDC.

You may ask why dental nurse registration took so long to come to fruition, and it is sobering to reflect on the number of changes that dental nursing has seen since 1993 whilst the thorny issue of registration has been debated. It is important to remember that the introduction of compulsory registration and, as we will see, the concomitant raising of the status of dental nurses, was not

A brief recent history of statutory registration

- **1993** Report of the Nuffield Inquiry into the 'Training and Education of Personnel Auxiliary to Dentistry' concludes that dental nurses should be registered with the GDC
- **1994** BADN publishes response to the Nuffield Report in support of the proposal – other dental organisations also publish responses, not all of them in favour of dental nurse registration
- **1995** GDC publishes consultation document
- **1996** BADN publishes response to GDC document, again supporting dental nurse registration
- **1996** Dame Margaret Seward, then President of the GDC, calls together all interested organisations to discuss registration and forms the Dental Auxiliary Review Group (DARG)
- **1998** DARG publishes its report and concludes, as Nuffield did five years earlier, that dental nurses should be registered with the GDC
- **1999** GDC makes formal decision to register dental nurses and other DCP groups
- **2002** First report of the Shipman Inquiry
- **2005** Final report of the Shipman Inquiry
- **2006** The first dental nurse registers with GDC

viewed as a welcome move in some parts of the dental profession or indeed amongst dental nurses themselves. There was considerable opposition to it and to several aspects of registration. Overcoming such opposition, through debate, consensus and consultation, always takes time; responses to consultation need time to be considered, assembled, collated and discussed. However, no one can now argue that dental nurse registration was rushed through or was ill considered through lack of time and attention, and the registration step, once taken, means that things can never be as they were before.

What does registration mean?

When you register with the GDC, you are effectively licensed to work as a dental professional in the UK, and you are answerable to the GDC for your work and professional conduct. From 31 July 2008, no one has been allowed to work as a dental nurse in this country without GDC registration (unless they are enrolled on a recognised dental nursing training course).

As we have seen, the GDC has introduced this requirement as part of its remit to protect patients and safeguard their interests. Dental nurses wishing to be included in the register must demonstrate that they are qualified and that there are no health or character issues that would affect their fitness to work as a dental professional. Equally importantly, when nurses register they make a commitment to behave ethically and professionally, and to meet and uphold the standards of the profession outlined in the GDC's standards and guidance. They also make a commitment to keeping their knowledge and skills up to date too. As the GDC has said:

> All these are important to patients. They will no doubt be important to you too, as a professional. To register benefits everyone, and is something to be proud of.

Whether you are a dental nurse of many years' experience and standing or an individual new to the role and starting on the path of dental nursing as a career, the requirements of registration and thus of being a professional are worth taking some time to consider and revisiting from time to time. In this book I will be referring frequently to the GDC's guidance 'Standards for Dental Professionals'. This is your route map to professionalism and I commend it to you. Revisiting the standards from time to time and considering what they mean for you at different stages of your career will be time well spent.

CHAPTER 2

What is professionalism?

The whole business of professionalism and what it really means to be a professional has taxed academics and professionals for many years, and will continue to do so as ideas continue to evolve and the boundaries of what we describe as a profession continue to be pushed further. The word 'profession' itself is not easy to define, and these days the word trips off the tongue perhaps too easily. We might describe a well-paid footballer as a 'professional' just as much as a doctor or lawyer, and we might even pay the amateur cast of a play a compliment by saying that the cast was 'very professional'.

Perhaps in our quest to find out what it really means we should start with a dictionary definition. If we turn to the Internet for a definition (http://en.wiktionary.org/wiki/professional), a professional can be defined as someone who 'earns his living from a specified activity'; however, this might describe someone who undertakes such an activity (whatever it is) for money rather than for pleasure or as a hobby. It doesn't get to the heart of what makes a professional in most people's eyes.

If we look for an alternative definition, we find the following in the *Macmillan English Dictionary*:

professional¹ /prəˈfeʃnəl/ adj ★★★
1 relating to work that needs special skills and qualifications: *Every applicant is entitled to good professional advice.* ♦ *Teachers must be free to exercise their professional judgment.* **1a.** showing a high level of skill or training: *the firm with the most professional approach to marketing* ♦ **very / highly / thoroughly professional** *I congratulate you on a thoroughly professional job, done in difficult conditions.* **1b.** behaving in a correct way at work and doing your job well: *The whole cast was very professional and hard working in rehearsals.* ♦ *They want me to dress in a more professional way.* — opposite UNPROFESSIONAL

This definition appears to show that being 'professional' is a positive thing, and involves special skills. It also seems to link being professional with certain standards of behaviour. If we read further down the definition in the *MED* we find the following second meaning:

2 relating to a profession and its rules, standards, and arrangements: *professional qualifications/training ♦ professional organizations / bodies / associations*
2a. working in a profession: *managerial and professional employees*

What is interesting here is the idea that the profession has 'rules, standards, and arrangements'. It is just those rules, standards and arrangements laid down by the GDC which we will be examining in more detail in this book.

Another definition provided by Roberts[1] pulls together some of these ideas further. Although this is referring to language teaching and not dental nursing, the general principles are clearly relevant.

> A profession is seen to provide a specialized and valued service to the public; in theory, at least, it is accountable to the public interest or the conduct and performance of its members. A profession, therefore, typically has a governing body which establishes standards of entry, certification, conduct and performance, and which imposes sanctions against members who fail to meet the conditions for continued practice.

This definition would seem to reflect the new status of dental nurses. Few I hope would disagree that dental nurses provide an increasingly more specialised and valued service to the public, and that the governing body (here the GDC) has established appropriate standards. However, how the GDC will measure those standards, what sanctions it will impose in the future, and how it will impose them upon those who fail to meet the standards of conduct and performance, will develop over the coming years to reflect society's and government's expectations as well as those of the dental nursing profession. Yet the inescapable fact is that there must be sanctions in order to maintain and uphold the status and credibility of the profession.

Another interesting and lesser considered definition of 'profession' is 'a public commitment or avowal' or 'a declaration of belief, faith or of one's opinion'. It is generally accepted that membership of a profession carries with it a set of values that will be reflected in the way in which work is carried out and the ethical standards that are adhered to. Professionals, in accepting their status as professionals, commit to those values, and are reasonably expected to demonstrate those values in their behaviour, conduct and performance. Professor Robin Downie[2] has identified some of the values associated with professional status in a paper exploring the characteristics of professionals. He says:

> The professional provides a service based on a special relationship with those whom he or she serves. This relationship involves a special attitude of beneficence tempered with integrity. This includes fairness,

honesty and a bond based on legal and ethical rights and duties authorised by the professional institution and legalised by public esteem.

This might seem strong meat, but as we shall see it is of relevance to the professional dental nurse.

Professor David Morrell[3], reflecting on Downie's paper and in looking at professionalism specifically in the medical profession, has identified the hallmarks of professionalism as

- **Confidence**: The trust of patients needs to be earned.
- **Confidentiality**: Patient confidentiality must be respected.
- **Competence**: Doctors need to demonstrate competence.
- **Contract**: the unwritten contract with patients to provide the best appropriate care must be upheld.
- **Community care**: doctors should be prepared to serve the community they are contracted to care for.
- **Commitment**: being a professional involves a commitment beyond the 9 to 5, and has an impact on life outside work.

These seven hallmarks or principles were defined for doctors, and were debated and ratified at a British Medical Association conference some years ago. Some of them are perhaps less easily transferable to dental nursing, so for simplification I have suggested the following four principles below for dental nurses to consider. As we will see in later chapters, these four principles also appear in the standards set by the GDC for dental professionals.

The principles are:

- Competency
- Conduct
- Integrity
- Responsibility

The public have a right to expect high standards of performance from the professionals that they consult, and these must be actively demonstrated in order to earn the trust and confidence not just of patients, but of dentists and other dental care professionals too. If we accept this, then we also have to accept that the professional has a responsibility to make sure that their competence remains at a high standard after their initial training, through professional updating, CPD and through a professional approach to professional development planning.

Conduct

Patients and colleagues expect, not unreasonably, to be dealt with in a civil, courteous and confidential manner and with due respect. How we deal with patients (or indeed our colleagues) is not only important for our own personal reputation but for the image of the entire profession. It is a sad fact that one professional behaving badly or in a way deemed inappropriate to their professional standing can reflect badly on the profession as a whole, and at worst bring the whole dental nursing profession into disrepute. However, a professional's conduct extends beyond the walls of the practice or department, and professionals accept the responsibility that if they wish to be treated as such then they have to show high standards of behaviour in both their personal and professional lives.

Integrity

One of the first phrases that those who are training to be a solicitor are taught is this: 'A solicitor's word is his bond'. That level of integrity is not so distant from that expected of a dental professional and a dental nurse. Both patients and co-professionals need to be able to put faith in a dental nurse and be confident in trusting them implicitly. This is impossible if there is any question over their honesty and integrity.

Responsibility

Being a professional brings with it many responsibilities, and being aware of these is part of the role of the professional dental nurse. Some of these responsibilities are outlined above, but there are additional responsibilities, not least the duty of care to our employers and patients, to our colleagues and to our fellow professional dental nurses. There is also a responsibility to exercise our judgment and use our skills in the best interests of patients. In demonstrating our responsibilities we can in turn exercise our rights as a professional

The GDC has been quite explicit in its guidance on ethical responsibilities and on its website sets out the six principles of ethical practice for dental care professionals, or the principles of practice in dentistry. These will be explored in more depth in the coming chapters, with specific examples of what this means in practice. Here is the GDC's guidance, taken from its website[4]:

- **Putting patients' interests first and acting to protect them**
  This principle sets out dental professionals' responsibility to protect patients by, for example, maintaining GDC registration, working only within the scope of their knowledge and keeping accurate patient records.

- **Respecting patients' dignity and choices**
  This principle sets out the importance of treating patients with dignity and respect, being non-discriminatory and recognising the patients' responsibility for making decisions, giving them all the information they need to make decisions.

- **Protecting the confidentiality of patients' information**
  This principle sets out the need to treat information about patients as confidential, using it only for the purposes for which it was given. Dental professionals should also take steps to prevent accidental disclosure or unauthorised access to confidential information by keeping information secure at all times.

  In some limited circumstances disclosure of confidential patient information without consent may be justified in the public interest (for example to assist in the prevention or detection of a serious crime) or may be required by law or by Court order. Dental professionals should seek appropriate advice before disclosing information on this basis.

- **Cooperating with other members of the dental team and other healthcare colleagues in the interests of patients**
  This principle states that dental professionals should work cooperatively with colleagues and respect their role in the care of patients. Dental professionals should also treat colleagues fairly and without discrimination and communicate effectively and share knowledge and skills as necessary, in the interest of the patient.

- **Maintaining your professional knowledge and competence**
  Dental professionals should make sure that they keep their knowledge, skills and professional performance under continuous review and identify and understand their limitations as well as strengths. Dental professionals should make themselves aware of best practice in the fields that they work and provide a good standard of care based on available contemporary evidence and authoritative guidance. They should also make themselves aware of laws and regulations, which affect their work, premises, equipment and businesses, and comply with them.

- **Being trustworthy**
  Dental professionals should make sure that they justify the trust placed in them by their patients, the public and colleagues by acting honestly and fairly in all their professional and personal dealings.

Learning how to act professionally and reinforcing one's own professional behaviour in and outside the dental surgery is a key element in the wider picture of professionalism, and an important part of continuing professional development.

However, in addition to the four principles set out above, I suggest two further principles: those of courage and compassion. Courage may not be the first thing you think of when you consider professionalism, but professionals may need to make difficult choices at some points in their careers; this involves an element of courage, and indeed courage in one's convictions, and so I believe this is a quality which many professionals need to display from time to time.

The second quality – compassion – is sadly sometimes overlooked. It is a fact that dental nurses are dealing often with people feeling concerned, worried, unwell or vulnerable. A capacity for compassion, an ability to engage and empathise with what a patient is feeling, may in the view of many be an essential quality for all dental care professionals to develop. In the rush of busy practice, in the concentration of ensuring high-quality cross-infection control, in the pressure of providing efficient chairside assistance, patients as human beings, requiring care and compassion, and their central role in what dental care is all about, should never be forgotten.

So where are we in our search for the definition we started this chapter by seeking? We could do worse than this one proposed by Cruess *et al.*[5]:

Profession: An occupation whose core element is work based upon the mastery of a complex body of knowledge and skills. It is a vocation in which knowledge of some department of science or learning or the practice of an art founded upon it is used in the service of others. Its members are governed by codes of ethics and profess a commitment to competence, integrity and morality, altruism, and the promotion of the public good within their domain. These commitments form the basis of a social contract between a profession and society, which in return grants the profession a monopoly over the use of its knowledge base, the right to considerable autonomy in practice and the privilege of self-regulation. Professions and their members are accountable to those served and to society.

Let's look at this in the context of dental nursing. The dental nurse today has to master an ever-increasing quantity of skills and knowledge in an environment of rapidly changing technology. This knowledge is certainly used to the benefit of and in the service of others – the patients. Since 2008, the dental nurse has been governed by the code of ethics and standards laid down by the GDC and registration itself is a form of profession of commitment to the GDC's standards which incorporate competence, integrity, altruism and the promotion of the public good. The GDC, with whom you register, provides the forum for self-regulation of the dental nursing profession, and as a professional the dental nurse is now accountable to patients and society as a whole.

Being a professional isn't just about registering with the GDC and paying an annual registration fee. It is about everything we say and everything we do in our working lives, and as such needs to be taken seriously, wherever you are on your professional career path.

References

1. Roberts, J. (1998) *Language Teacher Education*. Arnold, London.
2. Downie, R. S. (1990) Professions and professionalism. *Journal of Philosophy of Education*, **24**(2).
3. Morrell, D. (2003) What is professionalism? *Catholic Medical Quarterly*, February.
4. Ethical guidance from the GDC can be viewed at http://www.gdc-uk.org/Current+registrant/Standards+for+Dental+Professionals/.
5. Cruess, S. R., Johnston, S. and Cruess, R. L. (2004) 'Profession': a working definition for medical educators. *Teaching and Learning in Medicine*, **16**(1), 74–6.

CHAPTER 3

A question of ethics

The subject of ethics in healthcare has been debated for thousands of years. As we have seen, patients expect certain standards from their professionals and place trust in them. We expect when we consult any professional that they will behave in a certain way and provide us with advice (and, if appropriate, care) which will be objective and in our best interests. We trust them to do this and feel that we can show them this level of trust because they are professionals and adhere to certain standards of conduct.

The GDC states:

> Justify the trust that your patients, the public and your colleagues have in you by always acting honestly and fairly.

It adds:

> Apply these principles to clinical and professional relationships, and any business or educational activities you are involved in.

This is a simple statement and one that is easy to understand. However, what we have to face is that sometimes choosing the right action in a given situation can be difficult. Although all of us perhaps like to believe we are always honest and always fair, there can be grey areas or more difficult situations where nurses need to use their judgement. In other words, we need to consider questions of ethics.

Professional ethics (as opposed to business ethics which we will look at briefly in a later chapter) relate to how people behave in relation to their chosen career. DCPs are expected to behave in a certain way and follow the specific code of conduct laid down by the GDC. This helps to guard against their actions bringing their profession into disrepute. However, ethics is more than just a way to behave in terms of some sort of code of manners. For example, this appeared in a pamphlet for hospital nurses entitled 'Ethics for nurses' published in the 1960s.

> Ward routine has a certain pattern to encourage respect for the doctor: he is always accompanied by the sister, the ward is quiet, he is never contradicted; and by various means he is shown to be a person of pre-eminent skill and wisdom.[1]

We might struggle to think of examples in hospitals today where the doctor routinely moves smoothly around an almost silent ward on his or her ward round accompanied by a quiet and respectful sister (and note the expectation that the doctor would be a man!). Times have changed and our expectations are different now. But we do not question that nurses in hospital should have ethics, even though our views on the 'proper' way to behave may have changed somewhat since the 1960s. We still expect that nurses will show respect for doctors, and conversely that doctors will show respect for nurses. In the dental practice most patients expect the dental nurse to show respect for the dentist, and indeed the dentist to show respect for the dental nurse.

Ethics is therefore more than just an accepted way of behaving; it is the conscious and unconscious application of rules or principles or values that should guide our professional decisions about the 'right' thing to do in a given situation. How often do we take time to reflect on our own values and philosophy or approach to patients? But how much does our application of our own philosophy and values affect how patients view us and the practice we work in?

Most dental nurses can expect to face difficult situations in terms of ethics at some point in their career. An ethical dilemma involves a situation that makes a person question what is the 'right' or 'wrong' thing to do. Ethical dilemmas make individuals think about their duties or responsibilities – and the way they feel about them. These dilemmas can be very complex and may not be easy to resolve, because these more complex ethical dilemmas involve a decision between two choices both of which may be 'right'. Following professional ethics can lead to personal dilemmas in the workplace. An example might be where a professional duty to 'whistle-blow' on a colleague conflicts with a sense of loyalty to a practice or indeed the individual themselves – perhaps the colleague is also a close friend. For instance, you might discover that a fellow nurse who is also a friend is doing something wrong. You have a duty to your employer to report it, but also feel a duty to be loyal to your friend in a situation that could lead to his or her dismissal.

Learning to deal with ethical dilemmas is the mark of a true professional – and may well form part of your personal development plan.

Ethical issues are rarely easy to deal with, and over the years a number of different tools have been developed to help people think through such situations and think consciously about the judgements they are making.

First there are three questions which can help when considering ethical judgements. These are:

- **Transparency**: do I mind others knowing what I have decided?
- **Effect**: whom does my decision affect or hurt?
- **Fairness**: would my decision be considered fair by those affected?

So, for example, if you chose to inform your employer about an associate dentist who is also your friend who had been taking money from the till you could go through this process:

- **Transparency**: do I mind others knowing that I have told the Principal that my friend has been stealing? I mind my friend knowing (it will wreck our friendship), but not my colleagues, as I think they will understand and think I have done the right thing.
- **Effect**: my decision hurts my friend and our relationship. If she loses her job it may also hurt her family, and it might jeopardise her entire career as a dentist. I would feel guilty about behaving 'shopped' her.
- **Fairness**: would my decision be considered fair by those affected? Probably not – my friend would expect me to be loyal to her. However, my colleagues would think I have been fair to them if the finger of suspicion has been pointing at them unfairly for some time.

If on the other hand you decided *not* to inform you employer you might go through this process:

- **Transparency**: do I mind others knowing that I have not told the Principal that my friend has been stealing? If others in the practice, including the Principal, find out that I knew and said nothing I would mind, as they may feel I have colluded in the theft and may not trust me any more.
- **Effect**: my decision hurts my employer and the practice as a whole. It also hurts my colleagues as they may be under suspicion if the thefts come to light. If money continues to go missing it may also hurt the patients if we have to increase fees to cover money lost through theft. It also hurts my feelings of self-worth in not coming forward about wrong-doing.
- **Fairness**: would my decision be considered fair by those affected? Probably not – my colleagues would not think it fair if they had been under suspicion for something they had not done and I had the information to exonerate them.

Exercise

What would you do in the example above?

Would your answer differ if:

(a) the colleague was a dental nurse rather than an associate dentist?
(b) If the colleague was the only breadwinner in the family?
(c) If the colleague was a relative rather than a friend?

In the example above I have chosen a simple (although not easy!) case of ethics involving a colleague. Ethics involving clinical decisions can require a slightly different approach, and I have described below two frameworks to help to deal with ethical issues in healthcare; we can see these at work in the GDC's Standards.

Beauchamp and Childress's Four Principles[2] is a widely used framework which allows room for judgement in the way we have seen above. The four principles are these:

- **Respect for autonomy**: this means respecting the decision-making capacities and abilities of autonomous persons, and enabling individuals to make reasoned informed choices. That respect needs to be maintained even if we believe the patient is making a decision that we would not make in their situation.
- **Beneficence**: this considers the balancing of benefits of treatment against the risks and costs of that treatment; the healthcare professional should act in a way that benefits the patient.
- **Non-maleficence**: this involves the idea that the health professional should avoid the causation of harm; the healthcare professional should not harm the patient. If treatment involves some harm, even minimal, that harm should not be disproportionate to the benefits of treatment.
- **Justice**: this means that benefits, risks and costs should be distributed fairly, and that patients in similar positions should be treated in a similar manner.

As we will see in the coming chapters, these principles run as a theme through the GDC's Standards for Dental Professionals.

The second framework that we can consider when faced with an ethical problem is the CARE framework[3]. This is particularly useful in helping to reflect on one's personal approach to an ethical problem.

- What are my **C**ore beliefs and how do they relate to this situation?
- How have I **A**cted in the past when faced with similar situations? (What do I like about what I have done, what do I not like?)
- What are the **R**easoned opinions of others about similar situations? (What does our culture say about this situation?)
- What has been the **E**xperience of others in the past when faced with similar situations? (What do I like about what they have done, what do I not like?)

Ethics are interwoven with professionalism and form part of the daily fabric for the professional dental nurse, whether they are part of the conscious or subconscious life of the practice or dental organisation. Ethical issues are often only considered actively when a dilemma occurs, but a consideration of ethics, personal and professional, and how they relate to the workplace in which nurses find themselves is a worthwhile development activity for all dental nurses.

References

1. Wray, H. (1962) (reprinted 1971) *Ethics for Nurses*. Macmillan Journals Limited, London.
2. Beauchamp, T. L. and Childress, J. F. (2001) *Principles of Biomedical Ethics*, 5th edn. Oxford University Press, Oxford.
3. Schneider, G. W. and Snell, L. (2001) CARE: an approach for teaching ethics in medicine. *Social Science and Medicine*, **51**, 1563–7.

CHAPTER 4

Patient-centred professionalism

In the next chapters, we will examine professionalism from three different aspects. We can look at professionalism as having three cornerstones: these are professionalism in the context of the patient, professionalism in the context of one's colleagues, and professionalism in the context of one's own behaviour, image and development. These three principles can be traced through all of the Standards for Dental Professionals. However, it is in many ways difficult to separate the three, as the implications of each of them have an impact on the other two.

The idea of patient-centred professionalism is not new. This chapter shares its title with a thought-provoking paper given as evidence in 2004 to a Royal College of Physicians Working Party on Medical Professionalism by Sir Donald Irvine, past President of the General Medical Council, and Chairman of the Picker Institute Europe. (The Picker Institute specialises in measuring patients' experiences of healthcare and professionals and uses this information to improve the provision of healthcare.) In his paper, Sir Donald made this point about patients and doctors, although he might just as well have made it about patients and dental professionals.

> Professionalism rests on the three pillars of expert knowledge and skill, ethicality and service to patients. Medicine today is in transition from a 'doctor-centred' to a 'patient-centred' culture of professional behaviour largely as a response to changing public expectations of doctors and of professions generally.
>
> ... If the medical profession is to enjoy the full trust of the public in future then it has to put patient-centred professionalism at the heart of its vision for the future. The realisation of that vision must become its first and overriding priority for individual practitioners and professional institutions...[1]

The phrase itself, 'patient-centred professionalism', might even sound quite glib – almost a sound bite. However, being patient-centred in the dental practice or department is often a hard thing to achieve on a day-to-day basis. Indeed, Philip Newsome in his book *The Patient-Centred Dental Practice*[2] underlines this point and describes his research into how many practices can get this wrong, their good intentions to be patient-centred misfiring.

Take this for example. A number of dental practices adopt a mission statement in order to focus their staff on the reasons for the dental practice's existence and to remind people of what they are trying to achieve. I have seen in dental practices on more than one occasion this mission statement:

Our aim is to provide you with the dental treatment and care that we would want to have ourselves.

At first sight this might seem a worthy and indeed aspirational aim. But stop and consider for a moment. Is such a statement *really* patient-centred? Is wanting patients to choose the sort of dental treatment the dental team would have *really* putting patients' interests first? I have no doubt that practices that devise and promote this sort of mission statement do so with the very best of intentions. The practice wants what it sees as the best options and the best care for all of its patients. However, it could possibly be misconstrued as a desire to force the practice's values and the personal choices of those who work there on its patients – however well-intentioned that desire may seem. What the dental professional believes to be the best option may not be in accord with what the patient thinks is the best option for a whole palette of reasons.

Wait a moment though. Surely as the experts, as the dental health professionals, we are there to advise patients, educate them, make recommendations and help them to make informed decisions about their dental care and health? Surely this is why patients come to us? And as the experts we have the information and expertise that they need? Well of course, the answer to those questions is 'yes'. Herein, however, lie the seeds of a major cause of concern for many healthcare professionals, that the course patients might choose is not necessarily the one that the professional would recommend or would themselves have chosen. It is, however, the patient that has to make the decision as to their healthcare and treatment, and that choice might be a source of frustration or concern for the dental professional.

So what then is being patient-centred and why does it matter? The good news is that we have the GDC's guidance to help us to work this out, so let us turn to their guidance for assistance. The GDC sets out the six principles by which dental professionals should work, and which they should

apply to all aspects of your work as a dental professional. It is your responsibility to apply the principles to your daily work, using your judgment in the light of the principles.

The core guidance 'Standards for Dental Professionals' is supported by five supplementary guidance documents, and in the coming chapters I will highlight key areas of this. However, all professional nurses are strongly advised to read this guidance for themselves.

The question of judgement is an important one. There are many occasions in practice where there is no clear right or wrong answer to a dilemma or problem. It is on those occasions that a dental professional needs to exercise his or her judgement, and be able to on a future occasion to justify the decision made to demonstrate that under the circumstances the course of action selected was appropriate and reasonable. No one expects dental nurses to be perfect and make the right decision all of the time – but you must be able to justify what you decided to do and what you did, by explaining how you used your judgment. In doing so you could adopt one of the frameworks outlined in Chapter 3.

The three standards which reflect most strongly this idea of patient-centred professionalism are:

- Putting patients' interests first and acting to protect them.
- Respecting patients' dignity and choices
- Protecting patients' confidential information

The key issue for dental professionals is how these can be put into practice. The importance of being *seen* to put these principles into practice from the patients' perspective was highlighted by Harry Cayton, Director for Patients and the Public at the Department of Health to the same working party to which Sir Donald Irvine gave evidence in 2004. In his evidence he said this:

> The first thing I must trust is competency. Having confidence in expertisc, that is clearly central, as is trust in confidentiality. But I think that modern patients are increasingly concerned about the manner in which they are treated, wanting respect and courtesy as well as kindness, with good communication and the understanding of options and with informed consent.

This has strong resonances in the GDC's principles. Let us look at each in turn.

Putting patients' interests first and acting to protect them

This is the first principle and really sets out the importance of the patient-centred approach. Putting patients' interests first means that their interests have to override those of your fellow teamworkers, your principal or manager, the practice as a whole, the commercial desirability of a course of action (whether it involves hoping that they will undertake a particular course of treatment or selling them a toothbrush) and your own interests. Patients (and fellow professionals!) would not expect a nurse to walk out halfway through an appointment because they have a bus to catch. This might seem obvious, but some of the other aspects of this principle are perhaps less so.

For many, being patient-centred is reflected in a desire to be as helpful as possible – this can mean explaining treatment to patients and answering their questions. As we will see below, this is part of the guidance. However, it is important that nurses retain very clear boundaries, and as the guidance says 'work within your knowledge, professional competence and physical abilities'. It is important to retain the trust of patients that nurses work fully within their field of competence and do not step over into another's area. So in putting patients' interests first this may mean disappointing a patient who has unrealistic expectations of you, such as wanting you to explain something outside the scope of your knowledge or recommend a particular course of treatment – even carry out some form of treatment. These boundaries are not always clear, and sometimes you may feel under a great deal of pressure, perhaps for example from a patient wanting definitive guidance and advice, but as the guidance from the GDC repeatedly says, if in doubt, seek advice. The ability and willingness to seek advice and check before proceeding rather than just going ahead and hoping, is for many the hallmark of a good professional.

The GDC also covers within this principle issues of communications and complaints. It covers the importance of not just keeping accurate records, but also ensuring that patients have easy access to their records. This encompasses two issues: being able to provide patients with appropriate clinical treatment based on good records, and also ensuring a level of patient involvement in their treatment by promoting a level of transparency in the records that are kept should patients request them.

Patients have a right to complain, and those that do have a complaint about their care or treatment have a right to expect 'a helpful response at the appropriate time'. In this context care may mean non-clinical care. Many patient complaints do not involve clinical treatment but reflect a greater concern about the way they are treated as individuals or the levels of customer care that they have experienced, or how they have been communicated with (or not as the case may be). This is perhaps reflected in Harry Cayton's view of the importance of how patients are treated as individuals as well as the level of clinical care that they receive. If we are honest, complaints are never particularly welcome, even though they can be an effective driver of improved standards, but patients must not feel that in making a complaint *they* are unwelcome.

The idea that patients should receive a helpful response may involve looking more closely at your practice's complaints procedure. It may be that the dental nurse is the first port of call for the patient and is therefore the one dealing with a complaint in the first instance, even if the dental nurse is not the person named as dealing with complaints in the practice's complaints handling procedure. Few patients would consider a helpful response as one which basically says 'It's not my responsibility to deal with complaints, it's the practice manager's, so you will have to wait until she gets back from holiday/lunch/shopping so that she can deal with it'. For most patients the appropriate time to have their complaint acknowledged (if not of course dealt with and investigated in full) is *now*, and the dental nurse would need to feel both competent and confident in dealing with acknowledging the emotions and feelings of an aggrieved or anxious patient in a professional manner.

This is one of the key areas for CPD identified by the GDC, and this marks how important dealing with complaints is so far as they are concerned. A profession, and by association the members of that profession, that is not prepared to listen to feedback and accept complaints from those it purports to serve cannot hope to obtain and maintain the trust of the public.

In addition to their individual responsibility to deal with complaints, however, professionals according to the guidance should 'make sure that there is an effective complaints procedure where you work and follow it at all times'. If there is no complaints procedure or you believe it to be ineffective then your duty as a professional is to raise this with others in the practice or organisation in which you work: your manager, the practice manager or the Principal. Having a complaints procedure is not enough. If you believe or have evidence that it is not working then you have a duty to raise this, and to do so in an appropriate way so that it has a chance of being taken seriously. This is not so easy and we will be exploring this situation in a later chapter.

One of the more difficult aspects of this part of the guidance is perhaps the realisation that there may be situations where patients' interests override your loyalty to and friendship with colleagues. The GDC is unequivocal about this. They state:

> If you believe that patients might be at risk because of your health, behaviour or professional performance, or that of a colleague, or because of any aspect of the clinical environment, you should take action.

This can be very difficult when your concern is about the behaviour perhaps of a long-standing colleague or a Principal, or where you believe there are extenuating circumstances for their behaviour – for example a colleague is under a great deal of stress. There is a dilemma for many people in a perceived undermining of the team relationships and causing relationship and communications difficulties within the team set against the requirements of the guidance. However, the principle remains the same. Putting the interests of the patient first is paramount and the professional must deal with the process of doing so in a professional, competent and positive way.

Case study

At the end of her last appointment for an extended course of treatment Miss Watson takes you aside and says at some length that she is not happy about the way her treatment costs were explained to her, and that she felt that the associate dealt with her in an off-hand way when she asked for an explanation. She says that she said this to the receptionist last time but nothing was done. You ask her how she would like to take things forward, and tell her that she could if she wishes make a complaint so that this can be looked into formally. Miss Watson looks blank and says she thought she had made a complaint but won't be coming back to the practice anyway. The associate is leaving at the end of the month and has had some personal problems. What should you do?

'Respect patients' dignity and choices'

The GDC makes it clear that patients should be treated politely and with respect, in recognition of their dignity and rights as individuals. So far as their choices are concerned, the guidance is firm and states that not only should valid consent be gained before providing personal care for a patient (not just physical treatment), but professionals should also **promote** patients' responsibility for making decisions about their bodies, their priorities and their care.

Informed consent means that patients must have received enough information to make the decision they are being asked to make. This information most importantly needs to be given in a way that patients can use, and dental professionals should satisfy themselves that the patient has understood what we have tried to communicate. How many treatment plans use technical language which is often unintelligible to patients? Technical language for the practice is jargon to the patient, and it is surprising how many dental terms slip into discussions with patients. We assume they know what we mean, and carry on in that assumption because the patient does not question us. However, it is an assertive patient that is prepared to tell us he or she does not understand. Many prefer to nod and acquiesce with what we are telling them and then seek clarification about treatment and its benefits from someone else – often the receptionist!

The guidance also puts an onus on the professional to find out what the patient wants to know as well as telling them what you think they ought to know.

The GDC makes clear that patients have a right to refuse to give consent for an investigation or treatment, and that if they do that decision should be respected – even if you do not agree with it. This is particularly important for care nurses and nurses who discuss treatment plans or are asked questions about treatment plans with patients after the dentist has gone through the treatment plan with them.

Special rules on informed consent apply to adults whom you think are not able to give informed consent, including those with special needs, and if you are not sure whether an adult can give informed consent you should consult another professional within the practice or your defence organisation.

Case study

You are the Principal's dental nurse. A new patient, Mr Patel, who is a local businessman, comes out to the reception desk when you are dealing with the receptionist and says he won't be booking the hygiene appointment that the associate dentist has told him he needs because he cannot see the point, and doesn't really understand why the dentist has referred him. What should you do?

'Protect the confidentiality of patients' information'

This part of the guidance is one of the better known aspects of ethical behaviour within the dental practice and perhaps the most discussed. If you are given information about a patient to help you provide care for them, by law you must keep the information confidential.

The law aside, from the patient's perspective confidentiality is highly important. Harry Cayton underlined the importance of trust in confidentiality in his evidence to the working party, and the GDC says 'Confidentiality is central to the relationship of trust between you and your patient'.

However, there are a few occasions when patient information must be disclosed (for example to other healthcare workers) and the dental professional is expected to explain to patients clearly the circumstances in which you might share information about them with others involved in their healthcare. This is of course something to which they need to give consent and they must have the opportunity to withhold permission for you to share information about them.

This confidentiality must be preserved even when using patient information for teaching or research or for project work for courses and qualifications. This means not just preserving anonymity wherever possible but also making sure that you take steps to preserve confidentiality when storing files on your PC or sending by email. Your project or research for example might only refer to Mrs X the patient, but if the folder on your PC refers to Mrs Wilson, you could be infringing confidentiality guidance, especially if the folder is not password protected or could be accessed by someone else.

The GDC is also clear on another area which is relevant to many practices. The GDC says 'Don't talk about patients where you can be overheard'. Many waiting rooms and reception areas are open-plan and particular attention needs to be paid when talking on the telephone or in person at the reception desk. A great deal can be gleaned from listening to only one side of a telephone conversation.

Very occasionally you may feel that you must disclose confidential information without consent in the public interest – for example if you believe that you would be preventing a crime from taking place or where a patient is putting their health and safety at serious risk. In such circumstances you should always try to persuade the patient to release such information themselves or to give consent to that information being released. If you still feel that you need to release the confidential information, then you should seek advice before doing so and be clear as to your reasons for wanting to release the information.

What this means for nurses

Being patient-centred is not easy. This chapter is not an exhaustive discussion of all the implications of the Standards for Dental Professionals but has been intended to highlight several key issues for nurses to reflect on. It would be unreasonable to expect any nurse, however experienced, to be completely familiar with this guidance and its implications immediately. Some aspects of the guidance may be more pertinent to some practice situations than others. Nurses are well-advised to read the general guidance and the supplementary guidance (available as downloads from the GDC website) in full.

However, there are other things to take into consideration. In reflecting on the guidance, if you feel that you need to update yourself in certain areas, whether in patient communication skills; communication and raising difficult topics with colleagues; or the nature of and gaining informed consent, then these areas should be added to your Personal Development Plan, outlining your proposed Continuing Professional Development activities. To further your knowledge and understanding of the guidance and these specific areas is, after all, helping you in your development as a professional – and we will be exploring that aspect of professionalism in a later chapter.

References

1. Evidence given to the Royal College of Physicians Working Party on Medical Professionalism 2004 can be viewed at http://www.rcplondon.ac.uk/wp/medprof/medprof_prog_041216.asp.
2. Newsome, P. (2001) *The Patient-Centred Dental Practice*. Better Dental Business Books, BDJ.

CHAPTER 5

The professional within the team

In this chapter we look more closely at professionalism in the context of one's colleagues – the role of the professional in the team. Perhaps more than any other profession, dentistry uses the words *team* and *teamwork* in describing the people who work in a practice. Dental practice websites almost invariably have a section on 'The Team' (often accompanied by an attractive photograph of a group of individuals within the practice), and many sites in their description of their practice promote the fact that teamwork is a very important part of the patient experience. Let us also not forget that one of the most important training programmes in dentistry of the last twenty years used as its title 'Teamwork'.

All well and good; there is a general sense then that teamworking is a good thing, but the uncomfortable question is this: how far is teamwork really explored or even demonstrated in dental practices? In reality it can be argued that the dental practice landscape is not necessarily one in which teamwork as it is defined outside of dentistry is particularly apparent. There is a whole host of complex reasons for this   historical, social, cultural and funding-related. Dentistry, in common with some other professions has for many years operated in a highly hierarchical fashion and these hierarchies have only recently been challenged. So I am going to begin this chapter, perhaps unusually, by acknowledging that the reality of the situation in some dental workplaces is that teamwork is not of the highest order. I make that assertion so that we can explore the professional requirements with a sense of realism and gain some insight into how the professional dental nurse can adhere to the GDC's standards ethically and reasonably in situations which are not always ideal.

That teamworking is important is evidenced by the fact that the GDC includes it as a tenet of professionalism. However, the crux of the matter for most nurses is that for professionals to work effectively as part of a team they need to be acknowledged and treated as professionals themselves by other members of the team. That is not always the case; sometimes this is because of behaviours exhibited by other team members, and sometimes this is because their own behaviour provokes a certain response in others. The professional as an individual an area that we will be examining in Chapter 6.

Harry Cayton (Director for Patients and the Public, Department of Health) in his evidence to the Royal College of Physicians' Working Party on medical professionalism in 2004 proposed this as an idea:

> A new professionalism could be defined not in terms of autonomy, but in terms of relationships. Relationships with knowledge; with colleagues; with patients; and with society. The qualities of professionalism would then derive not from what a doctor is, from self, but from how they behave in relation to others.[1]

Denise Chaffer, Director of Nursing at the Worthing & Southlands Hospitals NHS Trust, has provided her reflection on this subject thus:

> Part of professionalism should include greater development of team working and the development of learning organisation principles, such as openness, fair blame culture, and mutual trust for team members. One important aspect of health professional teamwork is their collective responsibilities to the public they serve, and they must always be prepared to act in the public interest. For example, if a health professional has concerns about another, there must be a clear 'whistle-blowing' or 'raising serious concerns' process.[2]

These ideas are reflected clearly in the GDC's Standards for Dental Professionals. The Standards state that a dental professional 'is responsible for co-operating with other members of the dental team and other healthcare colleagues in the interest of patients'.

So what is teamworking?

Before we look more closely at these requirements, it is probably sensible to define our terms. The World Health Organization's definition of teamwork is:

> Co-ordinated action carried out by two or more individuals jointly, concurrently or sequentially. It implies common agreed goals, clear awareness of and respect for others' roles and functions.

The GDC defines a dental team as

> the group of people who together provide care for a patient. Teamwork means working together to provide good-quality dental care.

Interestingly, neither refers to the 'collective responsibility' talked about by Denise Chaffer, although from a patient's perspective this might be expected.

Both of these definitions, however, accord well with some more general definitions of teamworking:

> Teams are groups of people with complementary skills who are committed to a common purpose and hold themselves mutually accountable for its achievement. Ideally, they develop a distinct identity and work together in a co-ordinated and mutually supportive way to fulfil their goal or purpose.[3]

This definition is taken from the construction industry, but I believe it is no less relevant for that. The Chartered Institute of Personnel and Development defines a team as

> a limited number of people who have shared objectives at work and who co-operate, on a permanent or temporary basis, to achieve those objectives in a way that allows each individual to make a distinctive contribution.

The CIPD goes on to say

> The gradual replacement of traditional hierarchical forms with flatter organisational structures, in which employees are expected to fill a variety of roles, has also played a part in the rise of the team.

This is where things get slightly trickier; in many practices the traditional hierarchical structure still exists, and the flatter structure – described by the CIPD – with a more keen awareness of the role and contribution of less senior players (in hierarchical terms) is less in evidence. The Advisory, Conciliation and Arbitration Service (ACAS) has on its website perhaps a more realistic view of the terminology:

> In a general sense people talk of teamwork when they want to emphasise the virtues of co-operation and the need to make use of the various strengths of employees.[4]

This realism is echoed by no less an organisation than the NHS National Patient Safety Agency, which says

> Teamwork cannot be expected to emerge naturally, so it is necessary to provide the facilities that will help groups of healthcare practitioners to become a good team.

In other words, teamwork is not automatic, so we have to work at it to make good teamworking happen.

The GDC has perhaps gone some way to help practices in developing effective teamwork by being specific about what makes an effective dental team: 'a good team', says the guidance, 'will have good leadership, clear, shared aims, and work together to achieve them; and different roles and responsibilities, and understand those roles and responsibilities'. In reality, in some dental organisations this is not yet the case. Roles and responsibilities are not necessarily clearly defined and this will inevitably cause problems when trying to understand responsibilities and the scope of individual roles. The wise dental care professional would do well to seek actively for aims and roles and responsibilities to be clarified if they are unsure about the scope of their work or their responsibilities within their work environment. Similarly there is evidence to suggest that a significant number of practices – even if they do have clear aims – have not conveyed these to the key people who are expected to deliver them – their dental teams.

The GDC offers further opinion on the characteristics of the professional within the team, and it is unequivocal about the value of teamworking as it sees it:

> Good dental care is delivered by a dental team. The quality of teamwork is closely linked to the quality of care the team provides. All members of the dental team contribute to the patient's experience of dental treatment, and all have a role to play in making the best possible contribution to patient care.

The Standards lay down quite clearly the sort of behaviour expected of the professional within the team environment. As a professional your responsibility is to:

- Cooperate with other team members and colleagues and respect their role in caring for patients.
- Treat all team members and other colleagues fairly and in line with the law. Do not discriminate against them.
- Communicate effectively and share your knowledge and skills with other team members and colleagues as necessary in the interests of patients. In all dealings with other team members and colleagues, make the interests of patients your first priority.

The GDC goes on to stipulate that:

> All members of the dental team who have to register with (the GDC) are individually responsible and accountable for their own actions and

for the treatment or processes which they carry out. **This includes your responsibility for cooperating with other team members in the best interests of patients**.

The emphasis is mine. No matter how difficult or frustrating other members of the team might be, dental professionals have a duty to make best efforts to rise above this and demonstrate their own cooperation and ability to work as part of a team in the interests of good patient care.

The challenges ahead

You as a reader may be fortunate to be working in a well-managed, forward-thinking environment which plans for and embraces change and has considered some of these issues. The dilemma many nurses face as a professional within the team is, I fear, being treated as such.

As we have seen, the dawn of this new era of the dental nurse as professional can be traced back to a time when dental care professionals were termed auxiliaries and were the subject of the highly influential Nuffield Report on the Education and Training of Personnel Auxiliary to Dentistry of 1993. This report made recommendations to increase the range of skills mix available to the dental team, with a dentist involving appropriately trained staff to increase efficiency and orientate services towards prevention. We have seen some of the effects of that report in the introduction of compulsory registration of dental nurses registration and the further development of the dental nursing training curriculum.

However, the increase in status of dental nurses as registered professionals may well be perceived as a threat to the professional status of others. In 2000 Pam Swain, then Executive Secretary of the British Dental Nurses Association, was quoted as saying

> Nurses are still waiting in the wings. The GDC has made the decision to introduce statutory registration and the qualification is changing to an NVQ, but legislation will take time. Meanwhile, we are still waiting for a change in attitude and a recognition that nurses are professionals too.

Whether that change has fully occurred is a matter for debate.

It is generally accepted that successful teams do not necessarily operate well with distinct hierarchies, although teams do need a leader. In a joint statement in 2006 the Royal College of Nursing (RCN) and the Royal College of Physicians of London (RCP) said this:

Teams will need to determine for themselves the most appropriate methods, models and designations, reflecting the particular needs of the service. Leadership roles should be assigned acknowledging the work that need to be undertaken, and recognising the educational background, experience and aptitude of team members – including acknowledgment that traditional roles are not always the most appropriate ones to lead delivery of optimal patient care.[5]

As professional demarcations begin to blur, we might expect some concerns to be raised and turf protection to become apparent. It is difficult for some professionals to let go some of the comfortable roles in which they have placed themselves over many years (and I include dental nurses in that statement).

This change process has been documented in other healthcare professions. In her fascinating paper 'Rethinking Professionalism: the first step for patient-focused care?' Jane Salvage tracks the process of change within the health professions generally:

> *The NHS Plan (2000)* and other recent government directives are built on an expectation that practice will change. 'Shifting the boundaries' or 'breaking down the barriers' between professions is assumed to be the major lever. Yet the absence of any comprehensive vision of a new professionalism, vastly reduces the likelihood of systemic changes occurring in practice.
>
> The NHS plan says 'the old hierarchical ways of working are giving way to more flexible team working between different clinical professionals.... The new approach will shatter the old demarcations which have held back staff and slowed down care.' In fact shifting the boundaries may or may not be a valuable thing to do; it is not a good or bad thing *per se*. It may or may not alter the power relations between the professionals involved.
>
> Substitution of one health worker with another means the same patient need or wish can be met by a different occupation, or the same service provided. It does not require a shift in power relations though it may help to provoke it.
>
> Innovation (excluding the introduction of new drugs or hard technologies) involves a new service development, meeting a new or unmet need, meeting an old need differently, or developing a new care pathway in which the need of the patient (or population) can be met by a different and usually wider configuration of traditional professionals and other service providers, often called 'teamwork'. It usually requires a shift in power relations.[6]

It is that shift, the giving up of power or status by some members of the practice team, which many believe over a period of time will be inevitable, and which will be an uncomfortable one for some, but which surely must happen if nurses are to be considered as professionals. In some ways it is within their own hands and that is a subject to be explored in the next chapter. However, the shift is one that we can all look forward to on a profession-wide, and practice or department level and which as professionals we need to be ready to manage. It may perhaps be seen and is anticipated by some most readily in the area of the Standards, which many nurses and practices are already finding an uncomfortable one to come to terms with.

Raising concerns

The dental nursing training curriculum explicitly states that dental nurses should be able to 'recognise and take appropriate action to help incompetent, impaired or unethical colleagues and their patients'. But what does this mean in practice? The GDC Standards provide more detail:

As a team member, you have a responsibility to raise any concern you have that patients might be at risk because of:

■ your own health, behaviour or professional performance;
■ the health, behaviour or professional performance of an employer or colleague within the team;
■ any aspect of the clinical environment; or
■ any action you have been asked to carry out that you believe conflicts with your main duty to put patients' interests first and act to protect them.

At first sight this might to some appear to cut across the idea of teamwork. Surely within teams one supports one's colleagues and the idea of mutuality or working as a team means that that support is clear and evident? However, the GDC is clear that the purpose of teamwork is the best interest of the patient and supporting or covering up for a colleague who is not able to or declines to provide good care for patients for whatever reason is not indicative of following the Standards. This can provide a real dilemma for many nurses, particularly if the actions or behaviour they are concerned about are those of a senior colleague, their employer or indeed a close friend. However, choosing to do nothing is not an option. See what the GDC says next:

You have a responsibility to do this whether or not you are in a position to control or influence the organisation within which you work.

This puts the onus on every individual, regardless of their place within the hierarchy or the team. The GDC appears not to distinguish between an act of omission and an act of commission, and the professional's first duty in this case must be to patients and their best interests.

However, the GDC goes on to say

> A supportive team will encourage its members to bring any concerns or difficulties they have to the team at an early stage, where they can often be sorted out.

In fact the GDC has clear and specific guidance for those in a management or supervisory role on this very subject (and this includes many Head or Senior Nurses and managers as well as dentists and employers) and puts a clear onus on them to ensure that they are providing an appropriate environment in which teamwork can prosper and concerns are raised in a sensible manner. The GDC makes it clear that managers should actively encourage people to raise concerns.

> If you employ, manage or lead a team, you should do the following.
>
> ■ Encourage all team members, including temporary team members, team members on different sites and locums, to raise concerns about the safety of patients, **including the risks that may be caused by the way in which the team works**.

Again the emphasis is mine. Concerns may be raised over the way in which the team works, and the GDC is advocating in this guidance two of the features of good teamwork: open, honest and direct communication and healthy and constructive feedback. The guidance continues with:

> ■ Support team members who raise concerns.
> ■ Take steps to deal with any problems in the standards and performance of the team.
> ■ Have systems in place for dealing supportively with problems in the health, behaviour or professional performance of team members.

These are clear guidelines for supervisors and managers and a useful checklist for team development within individual organisations. The GDC has more to say on the subject of management and the relevant sections in the Standards should be reviewed carefully. It is also easy to miss the fact that their responsibilities cover the actions of both registered and non-registered team members.

> As a registered dental professional, you are also responsible for the actions of any member of the team you lead or manage who delivers

care to the patient but who does not have to register with us (for example, receptionists and practice managers).

Make sure that unregistered members of the dental team working alongside you or under your supervision are familiar with 'Standards for Dental Professionals' and its supporting guidance, and follow it.

Judgement, however, must be exercised. At the introduction of registration, some practices seemed to believe that they would be operating in some sort of dental police state, with nurses checking up on hygienists and dentists and rushing to call the GDC at the first opportunity if they believe something is amiss. This of course was nonsense; what would have been more helpful was for practices to consider exactly what the mechanisms were for dealing with questions, anxieties and concerns within the practice so that all members of staff felt that they had a sensible and adult forum for discussing practice issues and concerns.

Case study

A junior recently qualified nurse who joined the practice a month ago has come to you, as head nurse, and said that she is worried about what the associate dentist she is working with is doing in terms of an aspect of cross-infection control, as it is different from what she has been used to in her previous practice. She mentioned it to the associate who told her not to worry and just get on with her work. The nurse also says that the associate seems to be under rather a lot of pressure at the moment as he is getting married in a few weeks' time; he has been rather short with her and with the patients on a couple of occasions. The nurse is rather worried and doesn't want to make a fuss or get anyone into trouble, but she is bothered about the cross-infection control procedures. What should you do?

For the individual professional dental nurse, it is important to remember a few basic principles. The purpose of raising concerns is first of all to clarify the situation and if appropriate to enable steps to be taken for the situation to be rectified. This is of course best done by raising your concern in your practice or department with a practice manager or the Principal, or if this is not appropriate (for example your concern is about something the Principal is doing) with another senior member of the practice or member of staff. If your concern is of a very serious nature then you can call your indemnity society for advice – but this is not a likely occurrence. It is important to remember too, that it is easy to get hold of the wrong end of the stick, or if you are new to a role (or even a surgery within a practice) to be introduced to clinical or management practices which may be unfamiliar and jump to a conclusion that it is therefore wrong or inappropriate. However, the other side of the coin is the assumption that what is happening must be right because the practice has always done it that way despite what you have just learned on a course or read in a journal...

If in doubt, the rule of thumb should be to ask. However, how you ask and how you raise your concerns is not something that many of us find easy to establish and even more difficult to achieve in a non-threatening and neutral way.

If all of this seems rather onerous, remember that the point of all of this is to act professionally in the best interests of the patient. Your responsibilities are to do the best you can under the circumstances and raise concerns in the way outlined above – and to seek advice where appropriate. However, your own professional teamworking skills will inevitably have an impact and effect on those working around you. Teams do not develop overnight and teamworking requires effort on everyone's part to be truly successful.

References

1. Evidence given to the Royal College of Physicians Working Party on Medical Professionalism 2004 can be viewed at http://www.rcplondon.ac.uk/wp/medprof/medprof_prog_041216.asp.
2. Report of the Director of Dental Public Heath can be viewed at http://www.gwent-ha.wales.nhs.uk/publications/phmreport/chapter15.pdf.
3. http://www.constructingexcellence.org.uk/resources/themes/internal/teamworking.jsp.
4. http://www.acas.org.uk/index.aspx?articleid=837.
5. *Teamworking in Primary Health Care*. Report of the Royal Pharmaceutical Society of Great Britain, 2000.
6. Salvage, J. (1992) *Rethinking Professionalism: the first step for patient-focused care?* Paper published by Institute for Public Policy Research.

CHAPTER 6

Professionalism and the individual

In the previous chapters we have examined the professional dental nurse in the context of patients, and the professional dental nurse in the context of the dental team. Now we look at the responsibilities that the professional dental nurse has to him or herself as a professional, and by association to the profession itself, as all dental nurses stand as representatives of their profession. Professionalism is at the heart of what it means to be a dental nurse, and the GDC in its guidance makes it clear that DCPs need to monitor their own professionalism and their own learning. It is important to consider reflective practice in the development of not just expertise and clinical skills but also attitudes and behaviour.

The professional as an individual is reflected in the final Standard set out by the GDC, encapsulated in two words – be trustworthy. As we saw earlier in this book, patients expect certain standards from their professionals and place trust in them. The GDC states:

> Justify the trust that your patients, the public and your colleagues have in you by always acting honestly and fairly.

It adds:

> Apply these principles to clinical and professional relationships, and any business or educational activities you are involved in.

Professional behaviour extends beyond the practice or department walls, however, and the GDC exhorts us to

> Maintain appropriate standards of personal behaviour in all walks of life so that patients have confidence in you and the public have confidence in the dental profession.

So what is meant by professional behaviour in and out of the work environment? Well, first of all must come the realisation that as a professional you are a representative of your profession and that people will associate you with dental nursing whatever environment they see you in. Your behaviour will reflect on all dental nurses and will be associated with other members of your chosen field. In order to trust you, people (both patients and colleagues) must feel that they are confident in your conduct and behaviour.

This extract from the General Medical Council's guidance on professional behaviour for medical students gives us an idea of the expectations people have of professionals. Although this is set out for medical students, dental nurses can apply the same principles.

> Students must be aware that their behaviour outside the clinical environment, including in their personal lives, may have an impact on their fitness to practise. Their behaviour at all times must justify the trust the public places in the medical profession.

Examples of unprofessional behaviour listed by the GMC as giving rise to concern include criminal convictions or cautions, alcohol consumption that affects clinical work or environment, assault or physical violence, bullying or abuse, lack of commitment to work, persistent rudeness to patients, colleagues or others, and unlawful discrimination. This is quite a list, and although some apply to the work environment others do not.

If we apply these to dental nursing, much of this comes down to a contract of trust between patients and professionals which I mentioned earlier in this book. As a patient I do not want to think that the nurse dealing with me in the surgery might be worse the wear for alcohol, or has a tendency towards violent or abusive responses to people they do not like. Public confidence must be maintained and dental nurses must do their best to uphold this confidence by earning both confidence and respect; through their qualifications and skills, certainly, but also their behaviour. From the point of view of colleagues and patients, you are your behaviour. What you do and say reflects the sort of person that you are.

Communications skills

Often the most obvious outward and visible sign of professional behaviour is the way that we communicate, and a major element of professionalism involves examining and reflecting on the way that we do this. One of the expectations of professionals is that they will have good communications skills. But do we communicate in an effective adult manner with due regard for other people? Are we abrupt and aggressive or are we concerned about saying the wrong thing and so more likely just to keep quiet, even when something concerns us? We already know that the Standards put an onus on dental nurses to raise concerns, but for the individual this can be difficult. We need to look therefore at how we communicate professionally, particularly in difficult situations.

For some, a difficult situation might involve dealing with aggressive patients; for others, it might involve raising concerns about certain practices in their workplace or about a colleague's performance. Whilst we might do our best to deal with such situations effectively, a lack of confidence in dealing with this sort of encounter, or not knowing the best ways of dealing with them, can put a great deal of pressure on everyone.

However, there are some simple communications tools which can help to develop professional communications. This does not mean that all patients will magically agree with us or never miss an appointment with the hygienist again, or that Principals will immediately see things from our point of view, but it does mean that we can develop communication skills which will in many cases help us deal more confidently with more situations we find difficult and achieve the best possible outcome under the circumstances.

Listening skills

Effective listening is probably one of the most important skills for a professional to develop. Although people spend more time listening than they spend on almost any other communication activity, many people never really learn to listen well. If we listen well our responses are more likely to be better considered. Some common poor listening habits include these. How many have you indulged in?

- **Not paying attention**: Listeners may get distracted or think of something else.
- **'Pseudolistening'**: This involves trying to look as though they are listening but not actually doing so. Such pretence may leave the speaker with the impression that the listener has heard some important information or instructions.
- **Rehearsing**: some people listen until they want to say something; then they stop listening and start working out what they are going to say, then wait for an opportunity to respond. This often results in missing important information.
- **Interrupting**: The listener does not wait for the speaker to complete what they are saying in order to question or give comment.
- **Hearing what is expected**: People frequently hear what they want to hear; they think they have heard what the speaker has to say and in fact miss the point completely. Alternatively, they might refuse to hear what they do not want to hear.

- **Feeling defensive**: The listener assumes that they know what the speaker's intention or why something was said or for various other reasons, so stop listening. They may even say – 'I have heard it all before'.

We can improve the effectiveness of our listening skills by adopting some of the following:

- **Encouraging**
  This involves verbal communications using phrases such as 'Tell me some more about...'; 'You were saying earlier...'; or 'Could you explain what happened?'; as well as using appropriate body language.
- **Checking**
  This involves making sure that you are getting the right message and understand what the person talking to you means or is feeling: 'You seem to be very frustrated by that'; 'Am I right in thinking you said...?'.
- **Clarification**
  This again is making sure that you have a clear picture of what is being communicated: 'I'm not sure I understand. Did you say...?'; 'Did this happen when...?'
- **Affirmation**
  This involves acknowledging the input of the other party and reassuring them of the positive input that they have made: 'Thank you for telling me because we want to put this right'; 'You have given me a lot of information, thank you'.
- **Empathy**
  Showing a level of empathy for the other person's view, stance or emotional response can aid the communications process: 'I understand that this is very worrying for you'; 'These situations can be very difficult – it must have caused you real concern'.
- **Probing**
  This means finding out more about or adding a depth of understanding to (as opposed to clarifying) something: 'Could you tell me little bit more about...?'; 'When exactly did that happen?'.
- **Summarising/paraphrase**
  This can be helpful to collect into a sentence or paragraph the main themes of a conversation or what someone has said: 'So there seem to be several things that are important to you, firstly...'; 'The treatment started well but then when the tooth broke you weren't expecting it to take so long to deal with'.
- **Pausing**
  It is often helpful to make sure that you have given time to someone to say all that they want to without jumping in.

Assertive communication

In any situation where two people are trying to communicate they both have certain needs and wants. Patients want (and need) to have their dental problems attended to and want to have it done as painlessly and conveniently as possible. Assertive communication is built around the concept of the rights, needs, desires, wants and opinions that we all have. In many cases these needs and wants may be in conflict (for example the receptionist cannot ensure every patient is seen the moment they require it and at the same time maintain a full appointment book for the dentist). As soon as a conflict or point of disagreement arises people have three choices in the way they decide to behave:

- aggressively
- passively
- assertively

Aggressive behaviour assumes that my rights, needs, wants etc. are more important than the other party's.

Passive behaviour assumes that the other party's rights, needs, wants etc. are more important than mine.

Assertive behaviour seeks to recognise the rights, needs, wants etc. of both parties and to reach a satisfactory outcome for both parties.

The behaviour choice that each person makes will affect the communication process considerably. None of these communication choices is necessarily right or wrong. All of them at one time or another may be appropriate. Communications difficulties arise for an individual, however, when they become trapped in a communications pattern such as aggressive or passive without the skills or ability to choose another communication mode. Thus, for example, the person consistently choosing a passive mode of communication may become frustrated and angry at the outcomes that they achieve for themselves, leading ultimately to a lack of self-esteem.

Assertive behaviour can be defined as

behaviour which aims to satisfy the needs and wants of both people involved (the win/win situation)

It is open, direct and honest communication which seeks to stand up for the rights, opinions, needs and desires of the individual whilst recognising and respecting the rights, opinions, needs and desires of others. (We can already see some reflection of the GDC's standards in this statement.)

Assertive behaviour is behaving in a way that attempts to meet your own needs (perhaps professional requirements such as making sure that patients have appropriate information so that they can make an informed choice over something) and the needs of others (the patient may want to get way quickly to pick up their children from school and may not relish a long explanation) – a compromise that is as fair as possible to both parties, appropriate, and where both sides can see and agree the other's point of view.

Assertiveness is therefore about acknowledging and maintaining both your rights and those of the people you are interacting with. As professionals we need to acknowledge the needs and feelings of our patients and colleagues. If you as a professional feel uncomfortable in a situation it is worth remembering that you have the right to say so.

There are therefore many professional advantages to using assertive behaviour. Many people find it helps them to communicate more effectively, defuse angry situations and disagree with people safely and without causing aggression. It can help to defuse aggressive behaviour in such a way that the aggressive patient or member of staff does not feel put down, or that their point of view has no validity.

By contrast, passive behaviour is failing to stand up for your (or the practice's!) rights, failing to get what you believe to be fair, or allowing inappropriate behaviour to go unchallenged. Sometimes we are passive to avoid what we perceive as an unpleasant confrontation, or because we confuse being passive with good customer care or good teamworking. However, passive behaviour can sometimes be seen as condoning something which is inappropriate or unprofessional and it is important to make sure that if you choose to be passive that this is an active choice and not one made through fear or apathy – and that you understand the consequences of the behaviour you have chosen to adopt. Raising concerns about other professionals is an essential part of the GDC's guidance (there is even additional guidance on this) and therefore examining your own behaviour and communications ability is an essential part of being a professional.

An assertiveness model

If you are in a situation where you need to raise a concern about something that is happening within your workplace, it can be helpful to think through how best to approach this. Effective communication in this sort of circumstance focuses on the behaviour of the person (what they are doing or what is happening) and not the individual or their personality (the sort of person that they are). People can change their behaviour, but are less likely to respond to an idea that they should change their personality! For example, someone may be shy, but you can reasonably ask them to exhibit appropriate professional behaviour by greeting patients in a friendly manner.

For those using assertiveness techniques for the first time, the 'three steps' model can be very useful. It is a three-step approach to dealing with a situation where your needs and wants may be different from someone else's and where you need to find a way forward acceptable to both sides. The technique is a simple one to learn and you can use it if necessary to raise a concern. It is important to remember that you are aiming for a win/win situation and the best possible outcome under the circumstances, not some sort of perfect solution or a way to get someone to agree with your point of view and abandon theirs. This means that there will inevitably be some negotiating. Make sure too that your body language is giving the right message and that you look assertive and not passive or even aggressive.

Step one: Show first of all you have considered the other person's point of view or what their interest really is. This involves not just parroting what they have said. If you are responding to something they have said, make sure that you have genuinely listened to them and understand what they are communicating. You can then paraphrase what they have said so that you can check that you have understood; better still, acknowledge their feelings.

Example 1

'I understand that you are very anxious to see the dentist before you go away at the weekend to get this problem sorted out'

OR

Example 2

'I realise that you feel that it is very important to run to time and not keep patients waiting.'

Step two: Explain your point of view. Avoid (if you can) using the word 'but'. It stops people listening as they think that you are simply going to ignore what they have just said.

Example 1

'The first appointment I have is for Friday morning.' (This sounds more positive and is more assertive than 'I don't have an appointment until Friday morning'.)

OR

Example 2

> 'My concern is that we are not giving patients enough time to ask questions about the treatment they are going to have and I am worried that some go away without really understanding what they have agreed to.'

Step three: Suggest an appropriate way forward. You want to move from confrontation to an agreed outcome and it is important to open the door to that. It provides a negotiating start point and a more sensible discussion between both parties.

Example 1

> 'And therefore I suggest I book you in for the first possible appointment so we can get this sorted out before you go on holiday.'

OR

Example 2

> 'So I'd like us to discuss at the next practice meeting a way where we can make sure the patients feel they have time to ask about what they need to know without compromising the appointment system in the surgery or timekeeping.'

Case study

While on a course, during the lunch break one of the other dental nurse participants tells you that at her practice some of the nurses regularly go out for a drink at lunchtime to the local pub and that a couple of the nurses often come back having had (in her opinion) rather too much to drink. One of the dentists at your practice sometimes refers patients to that practice for specialist treatment by a visiting specialist who brings in his own nurse, and thinks the service offered by the specialist is excellent. What should you do?

Issues, positions and interests

When dealing with a difficult situation, it is useful to identify the other party's **Issues** (problems/concerns), their **Positions** (what they are demanding or expect to see happen), and their **Interests** (What they are worried about or desire to happen).

Issue: topic or subject of dispute
Position: one party's solution to, or predicted outcome to that issue
Interest: one party's concern about an issue

It is important to try to identify the interest behind these fixed positions in order to negotiate a satisfactory outcome for both sides. An interest is just another word for a need/desire or concern.

Conflict resolution aims to move people away from fixed positions so that they can recognise their interests and negotiate to get satisfaction.

Example

Issue: My new crown was due to be fitted today, and I was expecting to have completed the treatment at this appointment.

Position: If the lab work is not ready there is no way I am going to pay the full fee.

Interest: I need my new crown before I go on holiday next week.

Exercise

Think of a situation where you can use this model. What might be the issue, position and interest involved?

None of these approaches may come naturally at first. Communication is a skill and like most skills improves with practice.

Developing good communication skills also requires a high level of self-awareness. Understanding your personal style of communicating will go a long way toward helping you to create a good and lasting professional impression on others.

Reflection

How do you think your colleagues and patients currently perceive you? Are there any changes to your behaviour and communications that you think you need to make to improve your image as a professional amongst these groups?

CHAPTER 7

The dental nurse as manager

The business of dentistry, management and ethics cannot be kept separate from each other. People at all levels inevitably face ethical decisions in their everyday working lives, and ethical issues arise in respect of management and finance, as well as in respect of clinical care.

Business ethics is the application of ethical values to business behaviour. It applies to all aspects of business and management conduct, from practice business plans and how dental businesses treat their suppliers and laboratories to how dentistry is sold and accounting practices. It applies to the conduct of individuals within a concern and to the conduct of the organisation as a whole. It is about how a practice does its business and how it behaves.

A practice's core values and codes of ethical behaviour should therefore underpin everything that it does. Just as society expects a certain standard of behaviour from individuals and professionals in particular, it also expects businesses, including dental practices, to abide by similar sorts of standards. People expect practices to look after their staff and deal with their customers or patients honestly.

In 2008, the GDC issued further guidance for those in management roles within dental organisations: 'Guidance on Principles of Management Responsibility. This succinct document contains guidance which is intended for anyone with a management responsibility, registered as a dentist or DCP or not. This will include some registered dental nurses acting as Head or Senior nurses or practice managers.

Some of this guidance reiterates standards already laid out within the other Standards already referred to. However, it looks at the responsibility of the dental care professional from a distinctly management perspective. Although you may not have the word 'manager' in your job title, if you manage or supervise other people within your dental workplace then this guidance applies to you and you should be aware of it.

Early on in the guidance the GDC reminds us that

> Because you are registered with us, you are personally responsible for justifying your actions to us.... This means that you have a professional responsibility to be prepared to justify your actions in your management role in dentistry, as well as in any clinical role.

In some ways this statement gives us a clue as to how this guidance will unfold, and it follows similar themes to the other guidance. For example, it states

> Make sure you work within your knowledge and competence as a director or manager. Use and keep up to date with guidance on the knowledge, skills and attitudes you need to carry out your role as a director or manager.

For those with management responsibilities, making sure then that you keep up to date with modern management thinking and techniques will inevitably form part of your CPD plan. However, it is not just management thinking that the GDC specifies, but also the legal responsibilities you may have in a management role.

> Be aware of your legal responsibilities as a director, owner or manager and make sure that you meet them.
> Understand and meet your legal and ethical responsibilities in relation to equality and diversity (valuing people's differences).

Not everyone is clear about the level, scope or extent of their management or directorial responsibilities. If you are not, it would be sensible to make sure that you find out. This is particularly important for directors of dental companies (whether on the board or not), as their legal exposure is extensive and a lack of knowledge can make them very vulnerable. In addition, legal requirements and legislation change with time, and it is imperative for professionals to keep updated in this area in the best interests of patients, their practice or organisation and the people who work there.

Management responsibilities extend not just to one's own work as a manager but also work that one delegates. In this section the GDC says

> If you delegate your management duties (that is, authorise someone else to carry them out), make sure that the person you delegate them to has the skills to do what you are asking them to do. You will still be responsible for... the overall management of the duties you have delegated.

You can delegate authority and responsibility for the task, but not the accountability for its results or the process of carrying it out.

The guidance returns to the theme of trustworthiness and probity in the next element of the guidance:

> Be open and honest in any financial and commercial dealings you are responsible for as a director, owner or manager.

Although not stated explicitly, this guidance, taken with the previous guidance notes, might imply that dental professionals have a duty to raise a concern over a lack of financial probity or dishonesty that comes to their attention. In fact, the manager has a professional duty to ensure that there is an effective system for people to be able to raise concerns about performance of both staff and the organisation itself, as we see here:

> Make sure that systems are in place in the organisation you work for to allow people to raise early concerns about the health, behaviour or professional performance of any staff you direct or manage, or about any part of the organisation's clinical or administrative environment. Make sure that you deal with these concerns quickly and effectively.

The tension that might sometimes exist between commercial considerations and good patient care comes to the fore in this part of the guidance, and the GDC is clear about the primary importance of the best interests of patients:

> Make sure that you do not put the interests of patients at risk by allowing financial or other targets to have a negative influence on the quality of care provided by the people you direct or manage.

Note that the GDC has not said that financial and other targets should not exist – only that they should not have a negative effect on patient care or affect it adversely.

Finally, the GDC makes this explicit:

> As a director, owner or manager within an organisation, you are in a position to influence the way in which the organisation works and the way in which the people within it work. You have a responsibility not only to follow the principles in 'Standards for Dental Professionals' yourself, but to promote them to other people within your organisation.

This is asking you to make sure that people you manage are familiar with 'Standards for Dental Professionals' and its supporting guidance. This can be done for example by regularly looking at the guidance as part of practice meetings or peer group discussions, or having copies available in the practice or as part of a staff handbook, by promoting it as part of your practice's induction, and by using elements of it as part of the benchmark of good performance in your appraisal system.

It seems clear that the GDC's Standards are intended as a serious blueprint for the running of professional dental organisations as well as individual professional behaviour and is putting a responsibility on managers at all levels to broadcast, promote and uphold professional standards.

CHAPTER 8

The continuing journey

Continuing Professional Development (CPD)

As a registered dental professional you have made a number of commitments; these are to your profession, your patients, your practice and yourself – and your commitment to CPD encompasses all of these.

What we need to accept is that the knowledge, skills and competence that dental nurses develop in their initial training, although extensive, will inevitably become outdated, for example through the development of new technologies and techniques, changes in legislation or changes in thinking, philosophy or the world around us. Professionals have a responsibility to keep up to date in the best interests of patients, and that will involve developing a personal culture of lifelong learning.

What is CPD?

There is an almost bewildering array of definitions of CPD. If we start with the Department of Health we can find this on their website:

Health care staff undertake continuing professional development (CPD) to affirm their professional competence.

This is all well and good, but what does it mean? If we stay in the health-care arena, the World Confederation for Physical Therapy offers us this:

[CPD is the] process through which individuals undertake learning, through a broad range of activities, that maintains, develops, and enhances skills and knowledge in order to improve performance in practice.[1]

If we move outside of healthcare and look at another profession entirely, we find this on the Architects Registration Board website:

Continuing professional development is the systematic maintenance, improvement and broadening of knowledge and skill and the development of personal qualities necessary for the execution of professional and technical duties throughout the practitioner's working life.

This brings in a new idea – that of developing personal qualities as well as skill and knowledge. As we can begin to see there is a variety of definitions of CPD across the professions but it is usually taken to mean learning activities, which update existing skills, knowledge and ability. It is an ongoing process, which will continue for as long as you are a professional, of acquiring and updating knowledge and skills throughout your professional life, but it relies on a proactive approach to learning. CPD is about developing and enhancing not just clinical skills but also communication, management and other behavioural skills, which we have discussed in the preceding chapters.

Continuing professional development is just that – continuing, and therefore needs to be planned. New technology, new research, new methods of working, changes in regulations and changes in the world around us – all need to be considered by the professional, and put under the spotlight the need for the constant updating of dental nurses' knowledge and skills in order to maintain their professional competence.

What is very important is that CPD requirements (in other words the areas in which you feel you should be updating your skills, knowledge and ability) should be identified as far as possible by you, on the basis of your personal needs, and within the context of the needs of the dental organisation and of patients. So, for example, there is little point in undertaking CPD in a clinical area which your practice does not offer and does not intend to offer, if you have no intention of leaving the practice in the near future.

So what does the GDC have to say about CPD?

The GDC provides the following guidance first of all on 'maintaining professional knowledge and competence'.

Recognise that your qualification for registration was the first stage in your professional education. Develop and update your knowledge and skills throughout your working life.

CPD is of course a requirement, but there are other good reasons for you to undertake CPD. You may have a desire to develop your professional knowledge and skills. Many people enjoy learning and retain a real curiosity for acquiring new information, skill and experience – and learning can be very rewarding.

You might wish to demonstrate your professional standing or use CPD to help you with your career development and your next move in dental nursing.

What CPD is not is a series of training courses or lectures which must be undertaken. It is a framework for learning which is driven by the professional, and this idea of CPD as a process rather than a series of training courses is underlined by the next element of the Standards, which states:

> Continuously review your knowledge, skills and professional performance. Reflect on them, and identify and understand your limits as well as your strengths.

Usually, most of us are too caught up in what we are doing day-to-day and getting to 5 o'clock to have a really good perspective on how well we are doing and the effect we are having on our colleagues and our patients, unless we make the time to do so. Similarly, without taking the time to reflect it is easy to get left behind in terms of what constitutes good practice and latest thinking in different aspects of our job. As professionals, we should stand back on a regular basis and reflect about such things as our aims, behaviour, level of confidence and performance, both clinical and non-clinical. This is what the GDC is expecting us to do as professionals. If we develop good skills in reflection it can help us to gain a greater insight and develop a more honest picture of ourselves and our abilities.

We need to hold up a mirror to ourselves to show us how we appear to other people, and how we work as part of our team – in fact all of the things which make us a professional. Using skills of self-reflection can also provide us with a greater understanding of what affects our own performance and professional progress. Finally, we can work out how to develop our skills, abilities and behaviour to achieve more professionally.

The GDC expects a professional to develop these skills of self-reflection and also puts the onus firmly on individuals to be pro-active and to take responsibility for their own development – and not expect the practice or the employer to work out development needs or organise appropriate development activities. Indeed, it says explicitly:

> *Find out* about current best practice in the fields in which you work. Provide a good standard of care based on available up-to-date evidence and reliable guidance.

Dental nurses need to think about where they can source this information. Reading professional journals is a good start. Keeping up to date with what is going on at the local postgraduate centre, making sure that they see the course flyers for CPDs arranged by the local DCP tutor, checking what arrangements the local PCT may have made, joining local professional groups, and looking at the advertisements in journals for courses, books and other programmes can all contribute to your fund of knowledge in this area and help you gain an idea of what issues are current and where you can go to find out more about them.

There are some areas where the GDC has specified that DCPs must show that they have undertaken a minimum amount of CPD, and these are set out below. Make sure though that you check their website relatively frequently as this may well change over time – the requirements are always posted there.

Verifiable and non-verifiable CPD

There are two basic types of professional development activity you can undertake: verifiable and non-verifiable. The GDC has provided advice on the minimum amount of CPD which you should be undertaking in each category over a five-year period. With all of your CPD you should aim to spread this out sensibly over the five years – in other words, do not try to complete all of the CPD requirements in six months. The aim of CPD is to stay up to date, not to complete a certain amount of activity in a minimum period!

What are the GDC's requirements?

All DCPs will be required to complete and record 150 hours of continuing professional development every five years, a third of which should be verifiable (50 hours). This requirement was introduced on 1 August 2008. CPD will be a condition of continued registration. This applies for all registrants, including those who work part-time or are retired DCPs who want to remain on the register.

Verifiable CPD is any learning activity which has:

- concise educational aims and objectives;
- clear anticipated outcomes;
- quality controls (i.e. there must be an opportunity for you to give feedback on what you think of it);
- documentary proof of your attendance/participation from an appropriate third party.

It is your responsibility to check with the course provider that the activity meets the educational criteria and to get a certificate. If you don't, you can't count the activity as verifiable. If you're not sure whether an activity meets all the criteria for verifiable CPD, you should check with the activity provider. If it doesn't meet every one of the four criteria, you will not be able to count it as verifiable although you will still be able to count it towards your general CPD.

Activities which are of benefit to your continuing professional development but which are self-directed – for example, journal reading – are general CPD.

DCPs study the same core subjects as dentists in every five-year cycle as compulsory CPD. These subjects are core knowledge areas for all dental professionals. They are:

- Medical emergencies (at least 10 hours per five-year cycle)
- Disinfection and decontamination (at least 5 hours per five-year cycle)
- Radiography and radiation protection (at least 5 hours per five-year cycle)

Verifiable CPD

Verifiable CPD is activity where you can provide evidence that the learning was relevant to your current or future career needs, and you can prove that it took place. Verifiable CPD does not have to be about attending courses; for example you can read dental nursing journals and complete a questionnaire to check your understanding of what you have read which is then marked and returned to you.

The GDC states that:

CPD may only be classed as verifiable if (a) it meets the Council's educational criteria for verifiable CPD and (b) the (DCP) is able to provide independent verification of attendance or participation (e.g. a course certificate). There is no such thing as automatic verifiable CPD.

You must keep records of the verifiable CPD undertaken and the certificates you gain carefully as you may be asked to produce them.

A way of recording your verifiable CPD is provided overleaf.

Example

Learning activity	One-day course on 'Professionalism for nurses'
Provider and format	UMD Professional Ltd
Date undertaken	3 November 2008
Time spent	6 hours
Aims and objectives of course	To provide an overview of the main elements of professionalism for dental nurses and an introduction to GDC Standards for Dental Professionals
Learning objectives (what I set out to learn)	To find out more about the extent of my responsibility to raise concerns and appropriate ways of doing this
What I learned	I gained a good overview of the Standards and understand now the extent of my responsibility as a DCP in whistle-blowing. I also feel more confident in communicating concerns to others in the practice
How I can use this	I can provide information to other more junior nurses in the practice on this issue, and can also ask with greater confidence about areas which I have concerns over or do not fully understand
What else I need to learn now	I need to read up on the GDC's further guidance in this area and discuss with the practice manager how the practice system for raising concerns works
How this relates to my PDP	I feel I have achieved what I needed to in this area of my PDP in relation to developing more assertive communication skills and knowledge about the GDC's Standards.

Non-verifiable CPD

Non-verifiable CPD is a learning activity which does not have a defined or specific learning outcome but which could reasonably be expected to contribute to your development as a professional. This would include, for example, general reading of professional journals; following nursing, professional and general dentistry matters in magazines and on websites; or discussions with colleagues in an informal setting (for example, learning about developments in nursing at nursing forums, and even informally networking with other DCPs). In the example above, the further action could be recorded as non-verifiable CPD (the reading of the further guidance and the discussion of the practice procedures).

You should keep a summary of these activities to demonstrate that you have undertaken them and could use something like the following format.

Example

Learning activity	Reading 'Principles of raising concerns'
Provider and format	GDC document downloaded from website
Date undertaken	1 December 2008
Time spent	1 hour
What I learned	The specific requirements for raising concerns and the extent of my responsibility within the practice
How I can use this	I now know what I need to do if I need to raise a concern and I can also advise other nurses in the practice who are not sure. I can also cover this area at induction for junior nurses
What else I need to learn now	If I am to advise other nurses I may need to develop some coaching skills

A cautionary word

A note of caution is in order. It is important that the CPD tail does not wag the dog, so to speak, and that training opportunities are chosen for their relevance to a dental nurse's learning needs, and not for their or the practice's convenience or because a course provides the requisite number of hours. Choosing CPD and training and development activities is of course relatively easy. Choosing the *right* training and development activities which will deliver the right results for the dental nurse is less easy, but following a few simple guidelines will help to ensure that the CPD that nurses do choose is as effective as it can be.

It is all too easy to start to select courses that are convenient and that you know you will enjoy. Professional development should be carried out in a planned way, with development events and courses being selected which will be the most advantageous to both the individual and the practice. Being truly effective in CPD means ensuring that you are undertaking the right CPD in the right way at the right time – and for the right reason.

Your CPD activity too should be properly measured and evaluated by you to make *sure* that it contributes positively towards your professional development. Yet training and CPD are still often a haphazard matter, with people attending courses (often the most expensive kind of training) with little thought as to how the skills and knowledge can be applied. This very often happens because it is not planned.

Planning your CPD – a guide to personal development planning

As we have seen, your dental nursing qualification marks not the end of your learning, but in many ways the beginning. Just as some people say you really learn to drive after you have passed your driving test and have thrown away the L-plates, what you encounter in your working life as a dental nurse will highlight areas you wish to explore further, or will uncover aspects of your work you find challenging and feel you want to know more about to widen or deepen your understanding. Being a professional dental nurse involves reflecting on your skills and abilities in all aspects of your work, from clinical competence to working as part of a team, and thinking about how you can develop them further. This is what CPD and personal development planning are all about.

A good Personal Development Plan (PDP) is an excellent tool to help you to work out how you can manage your further development in ways that will benefit you and the environment in which you work. This is your responsibility as a professional and no one else's. It does not have to be arduous, but it will involve a regular cycle of reflection, planning and recording, so that you can work out what CPD you should be undertaking.

A good PDP will therefore help you to manage your learning in ways that will help you to develop effectively. It is a useful method of recording your achievements, identifying strengths as well as any areas in which you need to improve, reflecting on your progress as a professional dental nurse, and setting clear goals and action plans for the future. The benefits of a clear PDP are that you gain a better understanding of what you are learning and how you are continuing to learn and it helps you to clarify the strengths and areas for development. A good PDP will also highlight areas of opportunity and help you to develop an ability to set yourself goals and action plans and evaluate progress towards their achievement. Working through this process will help you as a professional to become a more effective and confident self-directed learner.

However, for the CPD over which you have free choice to be useful, valuable and most of all effective, it is important that when choosing your CPD activities you make sure that you choose it on the basis of the outcome or result that you are hoping for – in other words, what the CPD activity is intended to achieve, rather than the number of hours it provides, who is running it or where a particular course is being held. Will your chosen activity give you the increased skills, confirmation of existing skills or greater knowledge that you are seeking?

To work this out, and to help you choose the right CPD for you, you should consider the following questions:

Five key questions in PDP planning

- Where are you now?
- Where do you want to get to?
- How will you get there?
- What is the right activity?
- Was it effective or did you learn what you needed to learn?

Assess where you are now

The first step is to take stock of where you are. What are your skills, abilities, preferences, experience and qualifications? What are the areas you find less easy and more challenging? These could be non-clinical areas, but still relevant to your work.

The role of the professional dental nurse, as we have seen, covers much more than clinical skills; most nurses in practice will find themselves using communication skills, teamworking skills, negotiating skills, selling skills, and customer care skills to name but a few! They are all part of most nurses' jobs. Many will also have some management or supervisory skills if they manage a team of other nurses.

Consider your job description and your role, and take stock of where you are. To help you to reflect on this you can employ a number of tools. You could carry out a SWOT analysis on yourself, thinking about your strengths (what you are good at), your weaknesses (what you are less good at or feel you need to improve), the opportunities available to you (a supportive family or employer, or opportunity to progress within the practice or develop a new skills such as implant nursing), and the threats that you might encounter in your learning (busy family life, dislike of formal learning, for example).

Sample SWOT analysis
- *Strengths*
  Quick learner
  Qualified five years
  Undertaken additional courses in implant nursing
  Good communicator with patients
  Good team worker
  Adaptable to different working styles of dentists
  Good at training junior nurses
  Up to date with cross-infection control techniques
- *Weaknesses*
  Dislike confrontation
  Find aggressive patients difficult to deal with
  Can find it difficult to prioritise
  Little management or supervisory experience
  Can get stressed when very busy
- *Opportunities*
  Principal keen to see me progress
  Possible further qualifications in sedation nursing available
  Supportive partner
  Member of local nurses group
  PCT resources available to me
  Practice undertaking BDA Good Practice scheme – I could get involved more
- *Threats*
  Time – have one child changing schools this year and need to support him
  Time management (see weaknesses)
  Principal undertaking postgraduate diploma and may not be able to offer much support
  No promotion opportunity to head nurse in current practice

You can also seek feedback from other people. How would your dentist complete a SWOT analysis on your skills? If you have appraisal or performance reviews in your practice, getting feedback via this route can be invaluable in determining the areas that you could develop. If not, you can always ask for more informal feedback. You can also seek feedback from your own colleagues or other groups you may belong to.

Alternatively, you could use some sort of questionnaire to work out where you are now. The example below (reprinted by permission of UMD Professional) is an example of such a questionnaire. It asks you to evaluate yourself in terms of two things – ability or skills (what you can do) and knowledge (what you know). Sometimes you may score yourself differently in these two areas. For example, you may know a lot of the theory of something but are not so good at putting it into practice (or vice versa!).

There is a scale of 1–3, indicating whether you don't feel you are sufficiently competent and confident in an area (1), through reasonably confident and competent (2), to very competent and confident (3). You will see some areas have been left blank; it is a good idea to work out the areas that you think are relevant to your professional practice as a dental nurse (if you have a job description this is a good place to start) and your dental practice or organisation that you work in. This is something you could do as a team, and in itself could be useful non-verifiable CPD!

What this will give you is an opportunity to consider what areas you feel you need more knowledge in (which could be gained from a lecture or a course or reading a book or article) and what areas you need more skills in (which could be gained by a more active approach to learning such as role play, shadowing someone else, or being coached by someone.

Self-Evaluation Questionnaire for Dental Nurses

Name: _____

Date completed:

Please select the option that most accurately reflects how you feel.

Using the following system please fill in the 'ability' and 'knowledge' boxes below.
- ●   I don't feel I know a lot/I am not confident I achieve this
- ●●   I feel my knowledge is adequate/I am reasonable at achieving this
- ●●●   I feel my knowledge is (very) good/I am good at achieving this

Self-management	Ability	Knowledge
Understanding professional behaviour		
Using my learning style		
Carry out a SWOT analysis on myself		
Setting objectives for learning		
Monitor and evaluate own performance		
Identifying own learning requirements		
Keeping up-to-date with journals		
Keeping up to date with dental nursing advances		
Creating a CPD plan		

Time management		
Solving problems		
Managing stress		
Making effective decisions		
Transparency in dealing with others		
Using judgement		
Prioritising		
Evaluating CPD effectiveness		

Clinical	**Ability**	**Knowledge**

Working in the team	Ability	Knowledge
Treating colleagues fairly		
Sharing information		
Create and maintain effective relationships with staff		
Treating people without discrimination		
Demonstrating flexibility		
Communicating assertively		
Raising concerns		
Giving feedback		
Challenging behaviour of others		
Demonstrating awareness of diversity issues		
Maintaining a positive attitude		
Demonstrating respect for others' points of view		

Working with patients	Ability	Knowledge
Gaining patients' trust		
Respecting patients' confidentiality		
Demonstrating integrity		
Demonstrating honesty		
Create and maintain effective relationships with patients		
Gaining consent		
Respecting patients' decisions		
Dealing with difficult patients		
Explaining dental care		
Finding out what patients want		

Demonstrating professional behaviour	Ability	Knowledge
Behaving ethically		
Being fair		
Promoting a positive image of dental nursing		
Providing a good example		
Promoting a positive image of the practice		

Communication	Ability	Knowledge
Information-giving		
Asking open questions		
Asking probing questions		
Effective listening		
Interpreting body language		
Effective written communication		
Raising issues with colleagues		
Raising issues with Principal or Partners		

Reflect on what this means

Take time to reflect on this. What is holding you back? What are you keen to find out more about? What areas of your work do you need to know more about and why? What areas of your work are changing and what do you need to do or know to respond to this? Sometimes you drive change, but more usually the world around us changes – patients become more demanding or technology moves forward and becomes more advanced – and you need to respond to this to analyse the different aspects of your personal and professional development. This stage helps you develop the skills of critical self-reflection and to build an idea of how you want to develop.

Where do you want to get to?

Only you can answer this question, but be aware that there are many factors to consider when finding the answer. Where is your CPD leading, and what are your longer-term aspirations? You should consider both professional and personal factors as well as time, your family circumstances and support, finance, and motivation, but your CPD plan should be looking to the future and your development as a professional. It is after all in your hands.

What do I need to learn or develop?

Working out what you need to learn is the starting point of choosing the right CPD – not simply seeing what courses are available. In many cases, the starting point of choosing training is seeing a course or programme advertised which looks attractive; the answer to the question posed above then becomes a justification for choosing a programme which is there at the right time at a convenient location, but which may not meet any identified need.

It is all too easy to think about what will happen on the course or training programme (the process of CPD) and less on what you will get out of it (the outcome). Training is not an end in itself, but a means to an end – and that end is whatever you have determined it should be. Do you want to have a greater or deeper level of knowledge about something? Do you want to gain a practical skill?

If you have a clear idea of the outcomes they are seeking you are more likely to choose the right CPD and ultimately gain far more from the training.

How will I make sure this happens?

This stage involves developing not just a goal but also an action plan to ensure you can take a structured approach to achieving it and that you can monitor your progress and look back to see what you have achieved over a period of time. An action plan will help you to structure what you are doing and keep track of your achievements. It must be reviewed at regular intervals to ensure that it remains relevant and realistic.

What is the right CPD activity?

Mention the terms *training* or *CPD* and courses and lectures often spring to mind. However, these are by no means the only ways to meet your CPD requirements. It is sometimes easier to think in terms of what people need to learn, so perhaps this question should be 'What is the right method of learning?'.

Learning, although most people do not think of it as such, goes on almost daily in many practices. The fact that it is informal does not meant that it is ineffective – in fact much informal learning can be more effective, and much more cost-effective, than courses. You do of course need to record this as non-verifiable CPD.

Courses and lectures may be the most appropriate way to learn for some but there are a number of other options available to you. However, an important question to ask yourself is whether what you need is knowledge-based or skills-based. Do you need more knowledge (e.g. understanding stock control or cross-infection control) or is it a skills-based need (being more assertive with patients, or selling skills)? Skills-based needs are more likely to be met by a more practical form of learning, perhaps some coaching by another member of the practice, rather than a lecture which is intended to impart knowledge. It is difficult to learn practical skills at a lecture, which is why few of us pass a driving test after being 'told' how to drive – we have to have some practical lessons first! Knowledge-based needs, on the other hand, can be met by the more traditional forms of training such as lectures, but can also be satisfied by reading journals and books, and by using some of the readily available CAL or open learning programmes.

Other ways to learn might include:

- Coaching – using day-to-day work or a project as a learning experience; this is an excellent way to acquire new skills.
- Shadowing – watching someone else doing every aspect of a job or activity.
- Reading – books and journals to gain knowledge.
- Role play – working through a situation with someone to increase skills or confidence.
- DVDs – to gain knowledge and sometimes skills if this is built in to the programme. These can often be borrowed from libraries, making it a more cost-effective activity than outright purchase.
- Study groups – to gain knowledge and skills in a peer group situation.

When choosing the right method of learning you also need to be aware of your preferred learning style.

Understanding your learning style

How people learn has been the subject of a great deal of research by educationalists, psychologists and training professionals over the last few decades. What most people agree on is that we all favour different ways of learning. Some of us like books and lectures, some have a more pragmatic approach, and some prefer learning by doing or watching. It is also widely accepted that your learning will be more effective if you are aware of your favoured learning style or styles and try to seek out learning opportunities which match your style. For example, someone who prefers an active 'hands-on' approach may not respond well to being asked to sit through a series of lectures – they are likely not to learn what they need to, as the method of learning (the lecture) does not match their preferred learning style which would best be met by a more active learning activity, such as a participative workshop or some role play.

In the 1970s, Peter Honey and Alan Mumford identified four main learning styles. Most of us have a blend of styles but one or two usually predominate. The styles are:

- The activist – who prefers learning by doing
- The reflector – who likes to reflect on the experience gained before drawing conclusions
- The theorist – who likes more formal and structured learning, such as lectures
- The pragmatist – who likes to see the immediate application of what has been learned

Taking all of these things into consideration, your preferred learning style and most importantly what you are aiming to learn, will help you to choose the right CPD activity, but also help you to answer the crucial question afterwards...

Has the CPD been effective?

If you have clear idea of what you want to get from the CPD activity you have chosen, it is easier to assess how well your chosen activity has met the objectives you have for learning. After any CPD activity there are some key questions you need to ask yourself – and record on your PDP.

- Did the activity meet the learning objectives I had set?
- How can I put what I have learned into practice?
- Do I need help (from the practice or others) to do this?

After an appropriate period you also need to assess whether you actually have put into practice what you have learned. This is after all the point of CPD – and if it makes no difference, what is the point of doing it in the first place?

All of this information can be captured as in the example overleaf.

Development planning can be a very personal and rewarding process – or it can be a process you go through because it is required by the GDC. The choice is yours. As the word 'development' suggests, personal development planning is something that happens over time. It isn't a last-minute thing. It is most effective when you take time to think about what you have learned and where you want to develop. Of course the GDC has laid down some compulsory aspects of CPD, but this does not do away with the need for good planning based on an objective analysis of your own strengths and weaknesses. Good CPD also focuses on 'learning' rather than 'training'. What matters most to you in career terms after all is what you have learned – not how many hours you sat at a course!

Personal development plan for Anne Nurse

What I need to learn	Proposed activity (course, reading etc.)	Target date	Cost	Verifiable or non-verifiable CPD and no. of hours?	Learning objective or desired outcome → p. 71
I need to be able to deal with aggressive patients more confidently	Half-day course on assertive communication with HD Training Ltd	I want to complete this by December 2008	£75	Verifiable CPD – 3 hours	I want to gain practical tools for dealing with patients who are being aggressive
...					

Date achieved	Outcome/evaluation/what I learned from the activity (completed after the activity)	How I will put this into practice/use this learning?	Further action needed?
15 December 2008	The course was very enlightening and I achieved my learning objective; I learned three methods of dealing with aggressive patients face-to-face	I can put this into practice with this type of patient, but I can also put the communication skills into practice when I need to get my point across better at practice meetings	I need to arrange some role play with my practice manager to practise the skills so I can gain more confidence
⋮			

Afterword

We live in exciting times. Dental nursing can be a rewarding and challenging career choice and, as we have seen, it allows you to use and develop many talents and abilities. The long-awaited registration of dental nurses in 2008 and with that their elevation to a professional status that not had hitherto been universally recognised represents not the end of a journey in professionalism but the beginning.

It is a journey which may at times be difficult and challenging, but should also be rewarding. The expectations that others have of dental nurses, and which dental nurses as professionals will have of themselves, will inevitably change, evolve and develop over time. Wherever you are on your journey, I wish you well.

Index